For my mother, whose love did not
end—it continues to shape me.

"And Jesus wept."

— *John 11:35 (KJV)*

grieve.
grow.
glow.

THE
JOURNEY
FROM
GRIEF TO GRACE

Kimberli A. Gross. M.A.

COPYRIGHT PAGE

ISBN: 979-8-9945679-1-3

Published by:
Celebrate Still
Westminster, Maryland

www.celebratestill.org
info@celebratestill.org

Printed in the United States of America

FOREWORD

As a licensed clinical social worker, I have encountered many approaches to grief and *grieve. grow. glow.* stands out for its ability to navigate the often-uncharted waters of loss and healing. I have had the privilege of journeying alongside Kimberli as she has navigated her own process and the development of Celebrate Still. In this book, Kimberli A. Gross invites us into her deeply personal narrative with a sincerity that speaks to anyone who has felt the heavy burden of grief. It resonates powerfully with those experiencing early grief, enduring grief, or the quiet sensation of feeling "behind."

In the first section, *grieve.*, Kimberli urges us to pause—to sit with our pain and embrace our emotions without judgment. This serves as a poignant reminder that grief is not a sign of weakness; rather, it is a testament to the love we have lost.

The second section, *grow.*, delves into the transformation that can follow survival. Kimberli fills a vital space between clinical terminology and personal experience. Growth is not presented as an escape from pain, but as an enriching engagement with life—one that includes intention, boundaries, and self-discovery.

In the final section, *glow.*, Kimberli offers a vision of life after loss— a life marked by alignment and meaningful choice. This section highlights the importance of discernment, guiding readers to embrace the wisdom that often emerges through grief.

Throughout *grieve. grow. glow.*, Kimberli's faith serves as a steady foundation—present and supportive—while allowing readers the freedom to define their own grief experiences. Her warm, direct tone reassures those who may feel isolated in their journeys. This book is not merely a manual; it is an invitation to engage deeply in the healing process, to honor the complexities of grief, and to hold space for joy alongside sorrow.

As you embark on this narrative journey, I encourage you to take Kimberli's hand and allow her words to guide you. There is profound beauty in the vulnerability of sharing our stories, and through *grieve. grow. glow.*, you will discover powerful tools to help navigate life after loss. May this book be your companion as you move toward healing, growth, and the gentle glow that rises from the shadows of grief.

Bridgette Threat, LCSW-C
Licensed Clinical Social Worker

AUTHOR'S NOTE

If you are holding this book, chances are you have lost someone—or something—you did not plan to live without.

I won't pretend to know your story, but I do know this: grief has a way of making us feel isolated, misunderstood, and rushed to heal before we are ready. This book is not here to hurry you. It is here to sit with you.

grieve. grow. glow. is not a formula or a timeline. It reflects twenty years of lived experience—of loss, faith, missteps, learning, and grace. It is both personal and purposeful. I share my story not because it is unique, but because it is familiar in ways many of us do not feel safe admitting.

This book is written to be read slowly. You don't need to agree with everything. You don't need to resonate with every page. Take what you need. Leave what you don't. Come back when you're ready.

Wherever you are in your journey—grieving, growing, or beginning to glow—you are welcome here.

With grace,

Kimberli

TABLE OF CONTENTS

The Journey from Grief to Grace

grieve. grow. glow.

Kimberli A. Gross

grieve

Before you read another word, breathe.

Whether you are in the earliest days of a fresh loss, anticipating the loss of someone you love, or carrying grief that has lingered longer than you expected—you are here, and here is where you are supposed to be. I don't have a magic wand or a crystal ball that can tell you when the hurting stops and joy begins. What I do have is my story, my prayers, and my promise that with time—and with both faith and tools—you can learn how to live again.

Grief is the overwhelming experience of losing someone or something you can never replace. And when it enters your life, it changes everything.

This part of the journey is not about progress, productivity, or getting better. It is about permission. Permission to feel what you feel without rushing it, fixing it, or explaining it away.

I was twenty-three years old when my mother passed away in April of 2004 after a brief battle with cancer. At that age, I didn't have language for what was happening to me. I only knew that my world had split in two: before her, and after her.

What I remember most from that season is guilt and anger. Guilt because I fell asleep for seven minutes. Just seven.

I had been fighting sleep all night, convinced that as long as I stayed awake, she would stay. I held her hand tightly, bargaining with my own body—and with God—to remain alert. I reminded God of every miracle I knew. Every story I had been taught to believe.

You parted the Red Sea.

You healed the woman with the issue of blood. You raised the dead.

God, if You are in fact that same God… If You do this, I'll do that.

I negotiated. I pleaded. I made promises I was ready to keep.

When sleep finally won around seven in the morning, she was gone before I woke up.

I woke suddenly, certain that it was my fault. I believed she would not have left if I hadn't gone to sleep.

That belief made sense to me at the time. It was grief logic—love trying to control loss. Years later, I came to understand a hard truth: my desires will never supersede God's will, no matter what I do. It was a tough lesson, and I doubt I would have learned it any other way.

And then there was anger—deep, unfiltered anger.

I was angry at God for not doing what I believed He could do. I was expecting the kind of miracle I had read about my entire life. The Red Sea parting. The woman with the issue of blood being healed. I believed with everything in me that God would intervene because I asked Him to. I begged. I negotiated. I promised my life, my service, my devotion—whatever He wanted—if He would just let her live.

But I was also angry at her.

Angry that she didn't know she was sick—or that she might have known and didn't tell me sooner. Angry that she didn't have a hunch and insist on finding out. She was a registered nurse. She should have known. This should not have been her story. And it should not have been mine.

And then there was the guilt for being angry at her at all—because how dare I be angry at the person I was grieving.

When the miracle didn't come, I was devastated beyond words. Hurt. Disappointed. Angry. Not just because she died, but because she was mine. My friend. My mom. My support. My cheerleader. My everything.

Her loss felt like abandonment, and I was left trying to make sense of a life that no longer felt safe.

The hardest part wasn't only missing her—it was realizing how much I didn't know. I was navigating womanhood without the woman who taught me everything. Every ache in my body sent me into panic. I demanded blood work, full examinations, reassurance.

Grief didn't just take my mother; it stole my sense of security. I became fearful of my own body, convinced loss was inevitable and waiting for me again.

People assumed I could return to normal. Back to leading worship and serving in ministry. Back to work. Back to living. I couldn't do any of it—and honestly, I didn't want to. Life had moved on, but I hadn't.

This was my first real introduction to loss. Not distant relatives. Not acquaintances.

Losing my mother was my first introduction to pain, and I didn't know how to hold it.

I shut down. I self-medicated.

Guilt, anger, fear, numbness, withdrawal, hypervigilance, and masking are not signs of weakness. I know that now—not only from what I lived, but from years of sitting with other people in theirs. They are common responses to profound loss. They are the ways grief tries to protect us when our world no longer feels safe.

The version of me that emerged after her death was shattered into a million pieces. Although I was known as the life of the party, I withdrew from gatherings and formed a dangerous closeness with my own thoughts. Depression didn't knock—it moved in and took over the master bedroom.

I showed up for work, but I was so heavily medicated by providers who knew how to numb but not how to heal, that I couldn't function. I fell asleep in staff meetings and felt disconnected from work I once loved. Self-medicating looked like going to the gravesite every single day and laying there for hours. It looked like drinking myself to sleep. It looked like antidepressants that did nothing antidepressant. It looked like pulling away from people. Crying constantly. Being cold. Numb. Disconnected. Doing the bare minimum to survive.

My faith didn't disappear—but it broke.

That night—the night my mother was transitioning—I prayed like my life depended on it, because it did. After she passed, my prayers became verbal reminders to God of how He had let me down.

I come from a long line of pastors, elders, ministers, evangelists, musicians—you name it. I knew church. I knew Scripture. I knew the language of faith. And because of that, I also knew what would happen if I said my thoughts out loud. My faith would be questioned. I would be shamed or condemned.

No one ever said it outright—but expectations have a way of being felt, even when they're unspoken.

So, I stayed silent.

Attending church became an obligation. Faith felt pointless. I believed in God, but I no longer trusted Him.

Support existed in theory, not in practice. I was surrounded by "I'm praying for you" and "Let me know if you need anything," but nothing tangible followed. In church spaces, there was an unspoken expectation that I would resume serving without acknowledging the gaping hole in my heart. At work, I was expected to return—literally—and perform at my best. Life didn't pause, even though mine had shattered.

And to be fair, I didn't know how to ask for something I didn't yet have language for. I didn't know what kind of help I needed. Two things can be true at the same time: people genuinely wanted to help, and I didn't know how to receive it. There was also a part of me that didn't want help at all—because the person who had helped me my entire life was gone, and no one else could replace that.

If this sounds familiar, you're not failing at grief—you're learning it in real time.

I eventually tried to get help. I opted for Christian therapists because I believed they would have a deep answer that would fix me. When that didn't work, I sought a non-Christian therapist, believing scientific knowledge might succeed where prayer hadn't. I didn't know then what I know now. I didn't need to be fixed. I can say that now with certainty. I needed someone skilled enough to hold space for the space I was existing in.

I went to a white Christian therapist because I believed our shared faith would be enough to guide the work. But while the intention was good, the approach didn't account for my lived experience— my culture, my grief, or the complexity of what I was carrying.

I then sought out a Black Christian therapist, believing cultural understanding would bridge the gap. And while there was familiarity and care, the level of training needed to support the depth of my loss wasn't there.

Both choices came from a sincere desire to heal. Neither was wrong. They were simply unmatched for the season and the kind of support I needed.

I then went to a non-Christian therapist who wanted to start at the beginning of my life, when what I needed was support for the crisis I was actively living through. I wasn't avoiding my past—I was drowning in my present.

I was later referred to a psychiatrist who handed me prescriptions and sent me back into the same loop. Medication became the response, not the support. It numbed the pain, but it didn't teach me how to carry it.

That experience taught me that not every therapist is the right therapist—and that finding the right support is as important as seeking help. I couldn't pray this away. Not solely. I needed faith and knowledge. Belief and intentionality. I didn't know it then, but what I needed was a today version of me.

Even my family—who loved me deeply—couldn't help much either. We all lost the same person, but not the same relationship. Each of us was grieving a different version of her while carrying our own pain. We were hurting at the same time, yet in isolation—pretending, surviving, doing the best we could with what we had. Looking back, I wish we had pulled closer together instead of retreating inward. But none of us knew how.

So, I learned to mask.

Masking protected me from burdening others. From people's discomfort. From being told to be strong when I wasn't. In our homes and in our communities—especially Black communities—we acknowledge death, but we don't normalize grief. Everyone shows up with pound cake, rotisserie chicken, and sodas...until you leave the cemetery. They ask the questions—Was she sick long? Who got the body? How's the family? Why we ask these invasive, inconsiderate questions will forever baffle me, but here we are. They seem harmless, but in reality, we simply don't know how to allow our presence to be enough.

And then the silence sets in.

That silence opens the door for reality. I became a master at hiding my pain.

If any part of this sounds familiar, let me say this clearly: you are not broken. You are grieving.

"YOU ARE NOT BROKEN. YOU ARE GRIEVING."

If I could sit with that shattered version of myself now, I would tell her this: it's okay. Take the time to heal. It's painful. It's lonely. But it does get better—and you will heal. Crying is a human response to a human experience. Even Jesus wept. And after He wept, He gathered Himself and continued His work.

The same applies here.

Grief does not disappear, but it does change. This is not where the story ends. This is simply where awareness begins—and where the long, quiet work of growth can start.

grow

"GROWTH DID
NOT ARRIVE AS
CLARITY OR
CONFIDENCE. IT
ARRIVED AS
EXHAUSTION."

Growth did not arrive for me as clarity or confidence. It arrived as exhaustion.

Looking back now, I understand that exhaustion wasn't failure—it was information.

I don't remember a specific moment when I decided I couldn't live the way I was living. I just knew I was tired. Tired of feeling like an orphan. Tired of crying. Tired of spending my days at the cemetery. Tired of masking my pain with things that never lasted. Tired of pretending. Tired of hiding. Tired of depression sitting with me at every meal. Tired of being unable to function. Tired of being tired.

At that point, antidepressants had become my lift. Not a cure—just a way to get through the day. I wasn't healed, but I was surviving.

It wasn't until I found out I was pregnant with my first son—almost two years after my mother passed—that I remembered what joy felt like. I still wasn't healed, but I could smile again, even if only briefly. Joy didn't return as freedom; it returned as memory. As possibility.

Mother's Day, however, remained brutal.

Each year felt like a public reminder of what I no longer had. Everyone had a mother— but me. I was tired of crying through a holiday that celebrated a role I could no longer access in the way that mattered most. I was tired of participating in something where my starting player was gone. I didn't know how to fix that pain—I only knew I couldn't keep reliving it the same way.

At that time, strength meant getting out of bed. Strength meant leaving the house. Strength meant making it through a day without crying. Not falling apart equaled success.

I know now that redefining strength was the first quiet shift toward growth.

I was trying my best—especially after becoming a mother. I was trying to be what I thought a good wife was supposed to be. What I thought a good mother was supposed to be. What I thought a functioning adult looked like. I didn't have language for healing yet—I only knew how to push through.

What I understand now is that pushing was how I survived before I knew how to tend.

I people pleased. I forced relationships. I held tightly to people I should have released. I believed strength meant endurance, not honesty. And still, something was happening beneath the surface. I was building capacity. Learning how to survive—even though I didn't yet know how to live.

The mask didn't come off during this season—it multiplied. And masking, while protective at first, eventually became heavy.

Somewhere along the way, I became a wife. Looking back, I can see how unhealed trauma leads to fast and unhealthy decisions. Marriage was one of them. I was pregnant, and marriage felt like the expected thing to do. I had always been a "do the expected thing" kind of child.

Getting married without my mother was hard. I didn't have my sounding board. My compass. The voice that would say, "That's normal—don't sweat it," or "Try it this way," or even, "Girl, your father does the same thing." Those moments mattered more than I realized—and they were gone.

Marriage triggered things I didn't know I had buried. The grief of losing my mother showed up as comparison, longing, and jealousy. I was jealous that my husband still had his mother. I tried to force a relationship with her, hoping to fill a space that could not be filled that way. I don't blame her. I don't blame him. We were all doing the best we could with what we had. I am responsible for my part.

Eventually, that marriage ended. Divorce added another layer of grief. Single motherhood followed—and with it, a new kind of absence. My mother had been a single mother for the first six years of my life. She had wisdom I needed. Experience I could have leaned into. And now it was gone.

It felt like being the new employee whose trainer retires before you get to ask a question. How do you navigate life with two small children? How do you hold onto your identity when you don't even realize you need to? I became consumed by my kids—because what else was there? And when I felt like I was failing, my mother's absence grew louder. Grief didn't stay behind me. It followed me.

"UNADDRESSED GRIEF DOESN'T FADE—IT RELOCATES."

Only later did I understand that unaddressed grief doesn't fade—it relocates.

It lived in my cluttered bedroom. My messy car. My disorganized everything. It became the fourth member of my household—present but unnamed. The problem was, I didn't know it was there. I didn't know how to identify it, contain it, or tend to it. I didn't know about tools. About reframing. About pausing, journaling, or setting boundaries. I didn't know any of the things I teach my clients now.

I didn't know healing was possible because I didn't know I needed healing—or what kind. Like Dory in *Finding Nemo*, I just kept swimming. When you don't have help, getting through can look a lot like getting better.

If this season of your life feels familiar, know this: surviving does not mean you've failed at healing. It means you adapted before you had access to tools.

I also grieved the life I didn't get to live.

The conversations my mother and I would have had. The laughter. The shift where I would have become one of her close friends. I wonder if I would have called her by her first name. I wonder if she would have laughed. And at the same time, I recognize this truth: the version of me writing this would not exist if she were still living. Celebrate Still would not exist. This community would not exist. And I would not be meeting you, the reader, right here.

Two truths can exist at the same time.

During that season, I began setting boundaries before I had language for them.

On Mother's Day, I stopped going to church. I stopped going to crowded restaurants. I didn't want pity hugs, expected tears, or performative sadness. Even on good years, resentment and jealousy could still surface. I needed space—not to hide, but to regulate.

So, my children and I created our own tradition. Parks. Playgrounds. Cookouts. Music and dance parties on the deck. Those days became ours. It worked—until it didn't.

Eventually, someone in spiritual authority condemned me for not attending church on Mother's Day, reducing my boundary to "being sad." That judgment came from a seat they had never sat in. They held spiritual knowledge, but lacked the lived perspective required to extend human empathy.

At the time, I wasn't as outspoken as I am now. I took it on the chin. And it hurt.

The turning point came unexpectedly.

I attended a Mother's Day brunch to support my best friend Christal, who was the keynote speaker. Shortly after arriving, I regretted my decision. The flowers. The photos.

The laughter. The joy. It was exasperating.

During her sermon, she referenced me—not to single me out, but to name something honest. She shared that she hadn't always known how to hold space for me when I spoke about missing my mother. It felt awkward for her because she hadn't lived it.

And that made sense.

That day, I realized something important: sympathy alone is not enough. Grief spaces require lived understanding. And I knew, in that moment, that if my mother were still alive, I would not be in this space. This work required more than sympathy—it required experience.

I prayed that day. Not the kind of prayer I grew up praying—but one that was honest, unsure, and necessary. I asked God for a space for people like me. People who felt like outcasts not because they were broken, but because no room had been designed for their reality.

That night, Celebrate Still was born.

But what followed was not accidental. It was intentional.

As the brunch continued year after year, I learned something I hadn't expected. People weren't only grieving their mothers. They were grieving loss—period. Parents. Children. Relationships. Marriages. Pets. Income. Stability. Identity. Grief didn't discriminate, and it didn't stay neatly contained to one story.

People kept coming. Stories kept coming. And that's when I realized this was bigger than anything my own grief had imagined.

By the fourth year, attendance had grown to over one hundred and twenty people, and only about twenty-five were familiar faces. That spoke volumes.

Pain has purpose. And even in opposition, there is opportunity—not for gain, but for growth. The real challenge is learning how to grow through it.

I want to be clear—not in a polished or performative way, but an honest one. When this journey began, I blamed God for my pain. I saw Him as the source of my loss, not my comfort. My prayers were filled with questions, frustration, and disappointment.

But over time, something shifted. Slowly. Gently.

I began to understand what Scripture teaches—that "all things work together for good to them that love God, to them who are the called according to his purpose" (Romans 8:28, KJV). Not because the loss felt good or made sense, but because God met me in the middle of what hurt and began shaping something meaningful from it.

I also came to understand another truth that once felt impossible: "It is good for me that I have been afflicted; that I might learn thy statutes" (Psalm 119:71, KJV). Not good because of the pain—but good because of what the pain taught me.

I wouldn't be honest if I didn't pause here to acknowledge this: the same God I once named as the source of my pain slowly revealed Himself as my source of healing and comfort. Not all at once. Not overnight. But faithfully, over time.

Growth, for me, meant deciding to finish the work.

I knew I didn't want to only share feelings or ideology. Lived experience mattered—but it wasn't enough on its own. I wanted language for what I had lived. Frameworks for what I felt. Tools for what I had survived. I wanted to be prepared, grounded, and responsible with the stories people were trusting me to hold.

I also carried a promise. The night before my mother transitioned, she made me promise I would finish my degree. At the time, I didn't know how or when—but I kept that promise. Years later, I completed my undergraduate degree. Then I took it a step further and earned my Master's degree. What began as obedience became preparation. What began as grief became grounding.

Grow looked like accepting that life would never return to what it once was—and choosing to build something new within the space that remained. Healing wasn't about reclaiming the old version of my life; it was about creating a sustainable one for the woman I was becoming.

Celebrate Still became the result of my grow.

Creating it was different from everything else I had tried because it was community—a room full of people who understood the shoes I was wearing. People who respected my yes and my no. People who understood that good intentions don't always translate to good support, and that protecting my peace sometimes meant saying no.

It felt life-giving instead of draining because I found my tribe. And life makes more sense when you are surrounded by people who get you.

Before Celebrate Still gave anything to anyone else, it gave me purpose. It gave me energy. It gave me the desire to share my story so others would know grief is okay. The desire to help people grieve in healthy ways and reclaim time they didn't have to lose.

The desire to speak hope to single mothers, divorced women, and anyone living a life that looks nothing like the one they envisioned. The desire to remind you, the reader, that detours are not disqualifications—and that even here, even now, it is all somehow working together for your good.

And the desire to be healed, so I could authentically walk alongside others as they learn how to live again.

What began as survival eventually became intention. And intention, over time, became alignment.

glow

"A GLOW
DOESN'T
DEMAND TO BE
SEEN—IT
SIMPLY CASTS
LIGHT."

When I hear the word glow, I don't think of attention or aesthetics. I think of maturity.

A glow doesn't demand to be seen—it simply casts light. It rises quietly and touches everything around it.

Glow, for me, was the moment I realized I had put in the work and could finally live from it. I no longer needed permission to move differently.

Glow didn't arrive suddenly, and it didn't erase the hard days. There are still moments when tears come—but they no longer take over. I don't live stuck there. Glow means I'm intentional about applying what I learned in the growing.

My glow era is not about making it. It's about who I'm bringing on the journey with me. Glow is alignment. It's being in sync with purpose and vision. Alignment now governs my decisions—not urgency, not guilt, not expectation.

Glow is execution—the kind that comes from clarity, not chaos. It's where I live now.

Fully. Freely.

Living fully looks like creating and enforcing boundaries. I require clarity, capacity, and consent in my life now.

Living fully means understanding that no is a complete sentence—and I am not required to explain myself. It means building a life I actually love, not one that simply looks good on the outside. It also means giving myself grace when I fall short—because there are still moments when I do.

Those moments don't define me as a failure. They give me another opportunity to begin again—this time with experience.

Living fully also means authenticity. Finding my voice. Owning it.

I am no longer carrying shame—shame from missed marks, stumbles, or moments of rest. Not for the seven minutes I slept in the early morning hours of my mother's transition. Not for any other time when rest got the best of me.

What I know now is this: rest is not my enemy. I don't have to fight it. Rest restores me. It protects my mind. It shields me from burnout. It allows me to keep going without losing myself.

I am no longer carrying the need to do what's expected.

What I've learned about the God I serve is simple and steady: the only expectation that has consistently proven true is that God exceeds my expectations. The version of me driven by obligation and performance no longer exists.

Alignment now comes with two guiding questions:

Does this make sense for me—and does it make sense for this season?

Alignment looks like prayer. Like asking for direction. Like listening for peace, not applause.

Misalignment shows up as busyness—doing something just to say I did something. Staying active without intention. I can recognize it quickly now, and I no longer confuse movement with progress.

I learned this clearly through my work.

In my work, I've learned that alignment sometimes requires a pivot.

There are moments when something meaningful is also labor-intensive—and I've had to be honest about my capacity to execute it with care. Instead of pushing through out of obligation, I chose to pivot.

I offered something smaller. More intimate. Lower lift. Higher impact. And it was exactly what the moment—and the community—needed.

That's alignment.

Alignment isn't about doing more. It's about doing what makes sense for the season you're in—and for the people you're called to serve.

Execution in my glow era looks like reading the room.

Constantly scanning the crowd. Asking hard questions:

Are people seeing results? Are they staying?

Are they asking what's next—and do I have an answer?

It's not just about sold events. Outcomes matter. Impact is measured by connection, continuity, and care.

I've learned when to push and when to pause. When to hold space quietly and when to challenge gently. Some moments call for compassion—a hug, a tissue. Others call for laughter.

With clients—one-on-one or in groups—I've learned this: trust determines timing. Execution without trust isn't leadership. It's noise.

Seasonal awareness matters too. What is this moment carrying? What's the emotional weight in the room? Sensitivity is not weakness—it's wisdom.

Releasing guilt is easier now because I no longer negotiate with expectations that cost me peace.

Not every moment needs to be front-page news. Not every effort needs to be loud. I look for impact. For fulfillment. For the quiet satisfaction of knowing something mattered.

And that's what I want for you.

In your glow era, look for impact. Look for the quiet

fulfillment that tells you you're walking in purpose. Purpose isn't the finish line—it's the beginning. What you do with it is a marathon, not a sprint. There will be hurdles. There will be smooth stretches.

But you've already made it through the hardest part.

For me, the hardest part was losing my mother. I survived that. And because I survived that, I know I can survive anything.

Glow, for me, is also leadership—but not the kind that asks people to watch from a distance. It is leadership rooted in discernment.

I don't want people to simply observe me, because appearances can be deceiving. I want them to know I've walked in their shoes. Beyond losing my mother, I've lived through heartbreak, divorce, single motherhood, severed relationships—romantic and platonic— and all that comes with those spaces.

Grief is grief. And so is grace.

Grief is not my ending. It birthed something in me. It opened the door to a new beginning.

So welcome to my glow era.

I'm excitedly waiting for an invitation to yours. 🖤

A Benediction for the Journey

If you've made it this far, I hope you know this: you were never behind.

You were becoming.

Grief may have introduced itself without permission, but it did not come to destroy you. It came to reveal what was already inside of you—depth, compassion, resilience, and capacity you didn't know you had.

There is no timeline for healing. No checklist for joy.

No single way to grieve "correctly."

There is only honesty, intention, and the courage to keep going—sometimes slowly, sometimes boldly, always human.

You are allowed to grieve what was.

You are allowed to grow at your own pace.

And you are allowed to glow—fully, freely, and without guilt.

May you give yourself grace in every season. May you rest when your body asks.

May you trust alignment over urgency.

May you measure your life by impact, not performance.

And may you remember that grief does not disqualify you from joy—it may be the doorway to it.

This is not the end of your story.

It is simply the place where you choose how you will live next.

So, wherever you are on the journey—grieving, growing, or glowing—know this: You are not alone.

You are not broken.

And your light still matters.

With grace,

Kimberli A. Gross ♥

ABOUT THE AUTHOR

Kimberli A. Gross, M.A., is a grief coach, facilitator, and speaker, and the Founder and CEO of Celebrate Still, LLC, a Maryland-based organization dedicated to supporting individuals, families, and organizations as they navigate loss and change with honesty, compassion, and community.

With an academic foundation in **Organizational Management** and a Master's degree in **Human Services Counseling** with a focus in trauma and crisis response, Kimberli blends practical structure with compassionate, people-centered care. Her work integrates lived experience, professional training, and faith-based insight to create spaces where grief is normalized, healing is possible, and individuals are supported in building a new normal.
She is the creator of **Living Shattered**, a grief support program designed to meet people where they are while equipping them with practical tools to live fully again. Kimberli is known for her warm, relatable approach and her ability to hold both grief and grace without minimizing either.

Her work is rooted in one core belief: grief does not disqualify you from joy—it just may be the doorway to it.

Learn more at **www.celebratestill.org**

Follow **@celebratestill** on all social media platforms

Next Steps

If this book resonated with you, you don't have to stop here.

Celebrate Still offers grief support groups, workshops, community gatherings, and one-on-one coaching designed to help individuals move from survival to intentional living.

To explore current offerings, upcoming events, or support options, visit: www.celebratestill.org

You are not meant to grieve alone.

You've reached the end of this story—but not the end of your journey.

This book was written to offer understanding, language, and perspective around grief— how it shapes us, stretches us, and sometimes asks us to begin again in unfamiliar ways. If parts of this story resonated with you, that's not an accident. It's awareness.

If you're feeling called to slow down and spend more time reflecting on your own experience, there is a companion journal designed to meet you there.

grieve. grow. glow. — A 52-Week Guided Journey Through Grief, Growth, and Grace offers weekly reflections, affirmations, and gentle prompts for those who want space to process at their own pace.

You don't need to begin immediately. You don't need to commit to every page.

Your healing does not require urgency.

You may also find support in **Day by Day — Affirmations for Growing Through Grief with Grace**, a daily companion created for grounding, clarity, and emotional steadiness— especially on the days when reading feels like too much.

And if this is where you pause, let this be enough.

You've already done something meaningful by allowing yourself to read, reflect, and stay present with your story.

Wherever you go next—grieving, growing, or glowing— know this: you don't have to rush, and you don't have to walk alone.

A Moment to Reflect

You may want to write.

You may want to sit quietly.

This space is yours.

www.ingramcontent.com/pod-product-compliance
Lightning Source LLC
Chambersburg PA
CBHW050914120626
46552CB00004B/1564